ABSTRACT POURS

Mastering Acrylic Techniques for New Painters

Glenn Connie

Table of Contents

CHAPTER ONE

INTRODUCTION

In the event that you're amped up for getting to realize acrylic pouring procedures, we'll go over the rudiments of what acrylic pouring is and why it's so notable. So get your paints, cups, and material considering the way that right subsequent, you will not have the decision to quit thinking about the normal outcomes by and large! Acrylic pouring is a noteworthy methodology for getting your inventive energies siphoning and make something perfect. Expecting that you've never had a go at pouring acrylics, the going with acrylic pouring strategies for juveniles are perfect for you. Similarly, on the off chance that you're moreover developed, you can leap to the piece on cutting edge acrylic pouring methods they can be utilized as motivation or beginning stages for your own manifestations! We should make a jump.

ACRYLIC POURING SUPPLIES YOU COMPLETELY NEED

Before we progress forward to finding and rehearsing different pouring methodology, I'll rapidly remind you what we genuinely keep up with that ought to do in a pour painting.

Vital Acrylic pour supplies

1. A material (or another shape, or gesso board, or a wooden board) - I really suggest genuine and exceptional Blick materials.

2. Acrylic paint or acrylic pours paint.

3. Pouring medium.

4. 100% silicone oil to make cells: Impresa Pouring oil for gigantic cells or Impresa Silicone oil for various additional genuine cells.

5. Plastic cups and mix sticks.

6. Trash sacks or papers to safeguard your functioning region.

7. Acrylic sealer to protect completed pour.

8. Torch or a power weapon to crash bubbles.

Additional game plans

1. Palette edge (for swiping) - I utilize humble Conda edges for 2 prior years.

2. Sisal rope/string for String procedure

3. Gloves and cover to not wreck you.

4. Gesso, I use Liquitex Principal Gesso.

5. Squeeze holders to premix tones.

6. Tin foil sheet skillet to collect all streams.

7. Glitter for upgrades.

8. Hairdryer or straw for sprouting.

Expecting you feel overpowered, for the central undertaking simply purchase an organized to-utilize acrylic pouring set that typically coordinates every important hold, even cups! Here are lots of good choices for acrylic pouring packs for fledglings.

NEW POURING STRATEGIES SUPPLIES

The market is unendingly passing several new devices on to make our inventive excursion more straightforward. Not generally new things work better stood out from old school ones, yet I'm glad to share what I've found:

"Sprout" stainers for pouring, set of 3

The location Sprout pouring method

Addresses the material to lift it

What is an acrylic paint pouring medium?

A pouring medium is the clarification the appeal occurs, without it you will get no pouring coordinated effort in any capacity whatsoever. Basically, it is an extra substance that you add to your paint to increment acrylic paint stream and make liquid acrylic paint.

In any case, it doesn't work like water it isn't simply diminishing the paint. It keeps the variety lively and assists the paint with making great models. Essentially all eminent brands produce their spilling medium that works out decidedly for their paint. In any case, there are several top suggested pouring mediums: Floetrol,

Liquitex Pouring Medium, and Mind blowing GAC 800. To learn everything about pouring mediums and Floetrol, if nobody truly minds one way or another, read my full partner:

You utilize a pouring medium with standard acrylic paint to transform it into pour paint.

Every so often you can purchase as of now premixed paint for pouring, they reliably shouldn't stress over you to add any genuinely pouring medium, regardless! I'd in any case make them pour medium, as the paint consistency of premixed paint may not be wonderful.

CHAPTER TWO

ACRYLIC POURING RECIPE HOW TO THIN ACRYLIC PAINT FOR POURING

• Pouring recipe with Floetrol: 2 portions Floetrol to 1 region paint. Other than 2-4 drops of silicone oil for cells. Obviously half floetrol, 30% paint, 20% water + silicone oil.

• Pouring recipe with Unbelievable GAC 800: 2.5 teaspoons Astonishing GAC 800 to each paint cup.

• Pouring recipe with Liquitex Pouring Medium: 1 set aside tablespoon of paint to 1 cup of Liquitex Pouring Medium.

• Pouring recipe for cells with dish synthetic: add 2 drops of cleaning specialist in each premixed arrangement with pouring medium.

Acrylic Pouring Procedures That Look Perfect!

Here I will acclimate you with acrylic pouring procedures, some of them are more commonplace and simpler, and some of them need more practice and time.

That is the clarification I will isolate them into two parts: pouring frameworks for tenderfoots they are fundamental, fast to learn and require less unexpected supplies, and unquestionable level acrylic pouring techniques they could require some readiness.

The most outstanding acrylic pouring methods for adolescents are marble pour, dutch pour, sickening pour, and flip cup, once in a while got along with swipe technique and a hairdryer use. Amazing outcomes with scarcely adequate piece additional time you'll get with Swipe and String pull painting methods.

The most badly arranged critical level acrylic pouring procedure is Dutch Pour with Lacings: Shelee Craftsmanship philosophy.

All acrylic pouring procedures:

Acrylic pouring methods for amateurs

1. Traditional pour

2. Puddle pour

3. Dirty pour

4. Open cup

5. Flip cup

6. Flip and Drag

7. Spin

8. Dutch Pour (AirSwipe)

9. Marble Pour Method

10. Split cup pour

11. Kiss pour

12. Comb

13. Marble Rolling Pour

CRITICAL LEVEL ACRYLIC POURING FRAMEWORKS

1. Flower Pour Procedure

2. Cells with an arrive at edge

3. Tree Ring (Spin Pour) pouring procedure

4. Wing Pour

5. Swipe Technique

6. Ghost Pour

7. String Technique

8. Fractal Dendrites

9. SheleeArt Blossom Strategy (Dutch Pour with Lacings)

10. Balloon Plunge Pour

11. Dip Pour

12. Colander Pour

13. Funnel Pour

14. Wave Pour

15. Injection Pour

16. Internet Pour

17. Double Cup Pour

18. Multi-material Pour

19. Hammer Pour

20. Ripple Pouring

CLEAR ACRYLIC POURING STRATEGIES FOR FLEDGLINGS

1 - Standard Pour

The standard pour is the most un-mentioning approach with acrylic pouring for an adolescent, yet, it doesn't offer near puzzling impacts as other pouring techniques will do. You essentially need your premixed paint and the material.

RULES TO DO CUSTOMARY POUR PAINTING

1. Premix the variety in individual cups with pouring medium.

2. Add 2-3 drops of silicone oil to the cups to make cells (you can avoid this step).

3. Pour each variety independently on the material in lines, circles, any bearings and spots you'd like

4. Tilt the material and appreciate.

2-Puddle Pour Procedure

Utilizing the Puddle Pour procedure we pre-blend each tone independently and we pour them in a steady progression on the focal point of the surface. We for the most part pick one essential variety we pour first. Puddle pour is a conventional pour method and will be ideally suited for somebody who needs to start pouring.

THE PROPORTION TO PREMIX EACH TONE

Utilize fundamental acrylic pouring recipe 1 section standard paint to 1 section pouring medium or

2 sections liquid acrylic paints to 1 section pouring medium

To make cells we utilize 2-3 drops of silicone oil that we add to the cup. To get significantly more cells you can update your procedure and consolidate it with the Swipe pour strategy.

When all tones are poured, we move and slant the material surface to make the paint spread over the surface.

To create you're pouring considerably really fascinating you can make a large number "focuses" to pour, and furthermore utilize a brush handle to make a tail and blend paint before you begin shifting.

3 - Messy Pour Strategy (otherwise known as Grimy Pour Cup)

The messy pour technique is the point at which we premix each variety in a singular cup, yet prior to pouring it onto the material, we pour all premixed colors in a single cup, and afterward, we pour this blend on a superficial level.

CHAPTER THREE

THE MOST EFFECTIVE METHOD TO DO ACRYLIC POURING WITH FILTHY POUR CUP

1. Premix the variety in individual cup with pouring medium.

2. Add 2-3 drops of silicone oil to the cups to make cells (you can avoid this step).

3. Pour all tones in a single cup.

4. Pour on the material

To accomplish required impacts we will in any case move and slant the material.

4 - Open Cup Pour

With the open cup pouring procedure we do everything like for the Filthy cup, with the exception of we do it promptly on the material since we place a cup with cut-off base there!

It is smarter to have a cushion layer for this strategy.

1. Premix the variety in the singular cups with pouring medium and silicone (assuming you need cells).

2. Pour pad layer

3. Cup one cup in equal parts and spot over the pad layer

4. Pour all tones into this open cup. You will see the paint getting away from the cup it is alright!

5. Gently eliminate the cup and slant or twist the material.

5 - Flip Cup pouring strategy

The Flip Cup painting strategy is like Filthy Pouring: we blend each tone separately, pour all premixed colors in a single cup layering them, and afterward, we rapidly turn the cup down and put it in an upward direction on a superficial level.

To have a good time and cells, join the Flip cup method with the Swipe pour strategy (which expects something to swipe with)

STEP BY STEP INSTRUCTIONS TO DO FLIP CUP POURING

1. Premix variety with pouring medium and silicone oil (for cells) exclusively.

2. Pour all tones in a single cup, layering, without blending them.

3. Turn the cup down and put it on a superficial level does it rapidly!

4. Let it sit for several seconds to allow all paint to go down.

5. Carefully lift the cup up.

6. Add tones assuming that you really want.

7.   Tilt and move material until the entire surface and edges will be covered.

6 - Flip and Drag Pour Method

To hoist the flip strategy, you can drag the flipped cup across the material making a beautiful tail! This method makes one of a kind, liquid, entrancing plans and it is still simple and fledgling well disposed!

INSTRUCTIONS TO DO FLIP & DRAG CUP POURING

1. Premix variety with pouring medium and silicone oil (for cells) independently.

2. Pour all tones into one cup, layering, without blending them.

3. Apply pad layer (foundation tone)

4. Turn the cup down and put it on a superficial level does it rapidly!

5. Gently drag it making the bearings you need (wave, lines, whirls)

6. Carefully lift the cup up.

7. Add varieties assuming that you really want them.

8. Tilt and move the material until the entire surface and edges will be covered.

7 - Air Swipe (otherwise known as Dutch Pour) Strategy

Dutch Pour method is the outright champ assuming we discuss staggering and simple outcomes.

Furthermore, it is totally open for a total novice, this is the thing I like about pouring such a lot of room for inventiveness and you don't need to utilize a ton of troublesome strategies or modern supplies!

Dutch pour is frequently called the Air Swipe acrylic pouring method, as there is a normal Swipe strategy when we drag a level device over the paint to make cells, however with Air Swipe we use air a hairdryer is the most straightforward model that everybody has at home. The excellence of this strategy is there can't be two indistinguishable examples each new material will be incredibly exceptional!

Additional devices you might require:

• Hairdryer (you can likewise utilize a straw).

• Silicone is an unquestionable necessity.

INSTRUCTIONS TO DO DUTCH POUR

• Concerning Puddle pour of Flip cup, premix tones with pouring medium and silicone exclusively and afterward layer them in a single cup.

• Flip the cup onto the material and allow it to sit so all paint will go down. Try not to move the cup.

• Pour the foundation tone (negative tone) around the cup.

• Lift up the cup and ensure all the paint is on a superficial level, move the cup in the event that there is more paint left.

• Slant the material of let the tones as they are (in light of your thought nad inclinations try!).

• Utilize a hairdryer on cool settings to blow tones into the negative tone.

Dutch pour should be possible without flipping the cup you can add tone exclusively, framing lines, circles or some other shapes you like! Be inventive! I caution you against utilizing just water it doesn't tie the paint and influences the nature of the paint. I suggest utilizing pouring mediums, yet it's totally dependent upon you, obviously.

8 - Marble Pour Method

One of the most lovely, top rated, and most awesome strategies is the Marble pour strategy when we are essentially faking marble on our material. The base for this pouring procedure can be any of amateurs' acrylic pouring strategies, However, a few craftsmen guarantee that Flip cup is awesome for marble as it ensures the best mixing, which checks out.

However, this procedure is interesting on the grounds that you should be exceptionally cautious with acrylic pouring variety mixes: look into a genuine marble and attempt to remain at max 3 shades of a similar variety.

CHAPTER FOUR

INSTRUCTIONS TO DO FALSE MARBLE POUR

Pick references of regular or fake marble to get motivation.

1. Choose variety and its shades premix them with pouring medium (absolute 3 tones).

2. Pour 2 significant marble colors in a single cup.

3. Pour this cup onto the material pursuing the heading you need. Set the variety that will make lines that regular marble has.

4. Correct the edges if necessary, shifting

5. Take the "marble line" variety and make likes. Make lines go over edges and cross one another (take a gander at how normal marble lines go).

6. Tilt again delicately to make lines stream normally with different varieties.

On the other hand

1. Premix variety like for Flip Cup.

2. Flip and drag the cup across material.

3. Tilt (add more paint assuming a few regions stay revealed) and shake.

9 - Split cup pour

Part Cup Pour is about the right cup, unequivocally the new innovation that we have a unique split cup for acrylic pouring procedures. They can have from two to 5 segments and will assist you with making intriguing pours. A few craftsmen make Do-It-Yourself split cups with two segments by simply embedding a plastic sheet in a cut jug or a cup.

Additional provisions for Split cup pour a split cup of your decision!

The split cup is really simple to utilize in light of the fact that you premix each variety in a singular area, yet when you pour the paint, they will all come out together, blending and mixing! The split cup causes Wing to pour Simple in any event, for a fledgling, so you can give it a shot.

STEP BY STEP INSTRUCTIONS TO DO PART CUP POUR

1. Premix varieties with pouring medium in individual areas.

2. Start pouring! You can utilize round development as you do with Tree ring pours, yet presently you can move this way and that.

3.Once you've done pouring, slant the material to spread the paint. Done!

10 - Kiss Pour

Kiss pour is near a parted cup however you really have two cups you are pouring from simultaneously. Why it is called kiss pour? Since our cups are kissing

It is an astounding strategy to make a few dualistic plans, as in these two cups you can premix totally various ranges (like for messy cups).

11 - Brush Pouring Strategy

Brush pours are dreamlike they make such entrancing examples that you can't confuse this method with whatever else. At the point when you see a poured brush painting you think it is hard to do, yet as a matter of fact no.

How about we attempt

1. Premix all tones with the medium in individual cups

2. Get a customary hair brush prepared (obviously, it is smarter to utilize the one

you don't brush your hair with as paints can be very unsafe). How far the teeth are one from one more will impact the distance between lines in your pour, so you can explore different avenues regarding various brushes!

3. Pour all premixed colors into one major cup.

4. Pour the paint (you can do whirls, roundabout developments, flip cup or investigation)

5. "Brush" the paint with your brush making lines and waves:

12 - Twist Pour

This procedure is generally new and somebody genuinely virtuoso utilized turntables (indeed, the ones individuals use for cakes or stoneware) to make pouring! Regardless of what strategy you pick, you can turn as opposed to shifting.

Indeed, indeed, it can get untidy, yet it is such a lot of tomfoolery! The main thing you want is to purchase a turntable either turn inside an exceptionally enormous plastic compartment or "construct" a little wall around your material to ensure the paint will remain inside.

13 - Marble roll pour (also known as Upset marble)

Another simple yet imaginative pouring strategy is to utilize a weighty marble and allowed the ball to move across the poured paint, making totally staggering outcomes.

So you initially pour the cushion, then, at that point, premix and pour the varieties and afterward fail and shift the material like playing a Ball-in-a-labyrinth puzzle!

HIGH LEVEL ACRYLIC POURING METHODS

(Need somewhat more persistence and practice) In my arrangement, high level acrylic pouring procedures need either more experience and practice or a few additional provisions. As a general rule, high level acrylic pouring is for the individuals who feel great and have some control over the paint and its stream, ace different fundamental methods and have previously made some pour canvases previously, and are prepared to continue on!

14 - Swiping Cells with A Range Blade

There are just two sorts of individuals: the people who could do without cells and who need more cells.

While there are lots of recipes for making cells (even without silicone), there is likewise a rich procedure how to make cells pop in your pour with a range blade!

1. First, you really want a cushion layer

2. Then premixed colors with pouring medium go onto the material

3. Pour the cell activator onto a range.

4. Dip the range blade in it.

5. With a range blade delicately and rather leisurely swipe the paint, watching cells shaping. Astonishing method for waves. There are various shape and sizes of range blades and you can utilize any of them analyze!

6. After each swipe clean the blade with a towel and rehash stages 4 and 5 until you are content with your pour

7. You can leave it or slant and stretch the paint somewhat more if necessary

15 - Jug Base Puddle Pour: Learn Bloom Pour

Bottle Base Puddle Pour, likewise called the Bloom Pour strategy, needs an additional one apparatus the lower part of the plastic PET jug (size depends on you).

You will pour premixed colors in the middle on the jug base and paint stream will make bloom designs.

What you want:

• Plastic jug base or extraordinary Blossom cup stand.

STEP BY STEP INSTRUCTIONS TO DO BLOSSOM POUR

1. Premix the tones with pouring medium.

2. Place this contain base on the material legs.

3. Pour varieties in a steady progression in the focal point of the jug allowing them to run down on a superficial level.

4. When you accomplish wanted blossom design cautiously eliminate the jug base

5. Pour a variety in the middle (where the container base was).

6. Let it be, or utilizing a brush end makes impacts, or slant the material. You can likewise make it more unique utilizing a paper towel.

On the off chance that you need a foundation tone and extremely particular blossoms on it, pour foundation variety FIRST, before you place the container.

16 - Tree Ring Pour/Twirl Pour Strategy

With the Twirl acrylic pouring strategy or likewise called Tree Chime pour because of closeness, the paint is painstakingly applied to the material with roundabout developments, making an example that looks like the yearly rings of a tree.

Additional provisions:

• You can utilize a split blending cup for this strategy, yet it is discretionary.

CHAPTER FIVE

INSTRUCTIONS TO DO TREE RING ACRYLIC POUR PAINTING

1. Mix each tone independently with pouring medium.

2. Pour them, layer by layer, in one huge cup.

3. Start gradually pouring the paint moving your hand in minuscule circles, emulating tree rings. The developments ought to be delicate, slow and without a ton of room between them. You might need to begin at one edge and move gradually to another however a few

specialists likewise do it around and around.

4. Once it's finished, you again can shift the material to assist with painting spread around. Tree ring pours are hypnotizing to watch: paint streams and covers the whole material.

17 - Wing Pour Procedure

The Wing Pouring procedure is a changed Whirl Pouring, however this time we are attempting to emulate wings. To do so we want to make two reflected pours. It is one of the somewhat new acrylic pour methods and as the need might arise to get "wings" very symmetric and equivalent, it could be trying for a fledgling.

STEP BY STEP INSTRUCTIONS TO DO WING ACRYLIC POUR PAINTING

• Blend each variety you'll use in a singular cup.

• Then, at that point, you start layer the tones in a huge cup:

1. First goes the foundation tone, which will later show in the middle of between the wings

2. Then, pour the variety you need to be within the wings: you pour it on one side of the cup.

3. You can add a portion of the main tone once more it will make a difference when

you will pour. Be that as it may, it is discretionary.

4. Now you really want to pour in the cup a high-contrast variety all around just on one edge of the cup!

5. You can rehash stage 4 with however many tones as you wish. Every one of these variety will be outwardly of the wings. Assuming you do as such, add first in the middle between, to add more difference.

• Presently we can begin pouring:

• In the first place, raise the material on your side. You can utilize cups or unique lifting stands.

• Pour and spread the foundation tone.

• Begin pouring the paint blend in the center quarter in a steady even stream.

• You can lift delicately the material to make a long wing, however this step takes a ton of training and can undoubtedly demolish the entire thing.

As you see the interesting part is the cup and layering the varieties.

That is the reason numerous painters are attempting to concoct natively constructed devices and cups that will facilitate the cycle and assurance the wing pour to find lasting success.

One of those stunts is the Perfect partner strategy and another is somewhat cup in the cup framework.

18 - Swipe Pouring Method: We really want More cells!

The swipe pouring method (additionally called the cleaning procedure) can be utilized alone or joined with other pouring strategies.

The Swipe method makes bunches of cells and to do so we utilize a range blade or a material.

THE BEST STRATEGIES MIX IS PUDDLE POUR OR FLIP CUP PLUS SWIPE POUR

Additional provisions:

• Spatula or range blade (or even a piece of cardboard)

• Silicone is the unquestionable requirement in this strategy you can't skip it in the recipe!

STEP BY STEP INSTRUCTIONS TO DO SWIPE POUR

1. Premix varieties exclusively with pouring medium and silicone, and layer them like for Puddle Pour strategy.

2. Premix more paint with pouring medium yet without silicone in individual cups, don't blend in one cup.

3. Pour the paint with silicone on the material.

4. Pour the variety without silicon over it and utilizing a range blade or a spatula

drag the paint. You will see cells showing up!

5. Repeat until you like the outcomes.

On the other hand, you can simply apply the varieties separately on the material and afterward drag a piece of cardboard or a spatula across.

19 - Phantom Pour

The Phantom Pour strategy is a variety of the Swipe Pour procedure. With the Phantom pour, you swipe from the center of the material making reflected designs.

It tends to be regardless of cells, in view of your inclinations.

This strategy needs a piece of cardboard or something to swipe (range blade, plastic sheeting).

INSTRUCTIONS TO DO APPARITION POUR

1. Premix varieties exclusively with pouring medium and silicone oil, on the off chance that you need cells.

2. Pour and spread the negative tone (your experience).

3. Start pouring varieties one close to one more in the center of the material, making lines or circles (in light of your thought and motivation). You pour them at the point from where you'll swipe them in two inverse bearings. You can premix two

tones and white/dark and substitute the lines: gold, white, silver, white, and so forth.

4. Now to swiping! Ensure your swiping instrument is perfect and dry! Begin pulling the paint from the center towards the edge.

5. You can add more tone and swipe again until you like the result.

6. If you added silicone oil, use light to make cells apparent.

20 - String Pour Method (String Pull Pour/Chain Pull Strategy)

The string pours method entirely one or a few strings (like a sisal line) to make an example: a plume is the most famous plan you can make with a string.

String pour method is difficult in any way, it requires investment and practice.

Additional provisions:

• string (jute or making twine, or medium to thick yarn).

INSTRUCTIONS TO DO STRING PULL POUR

There are a few methodologies on the best way to do string pour: some absorb strings paint prior to pouring, some set the string on the right track and cover it with paint or don't. It doesn't actually have an effect it involves propensity and inclinations.

1. Premix each variety in a singular cup with pouring medium.

2. Pour foundation tone (negative tone) and spread it uniformly over the material.

3. Put 20-30 cm long strings in each tone and allowed them to splash the paint. However, try not to allow them to sit in paint combination excessively lengthy. Or on the other hand, on the other hand, you can place strings first in a cup and afterward layer all tones on top.

4. Take the primary string off the paint and layer it on the material: you can shape a roll yet not excessively thick or just crisscross lines. Rehash with all lines. Ensure the tail of each string is not

difficult to get to as a rule you will simply leave it looming over the material's edge.

21 - Fractal Dendrites Pour

The fractal dendrites pour procedure is one of the most gorgeous strategies when we make structures like fractals and dendrites with pouring and liquor.

We don't need to paint fractals ourselves, "nature" or, unequivocally liquor on the pour paint will make basically everything. When you let the primary let's fall down, you'll see the sorcery. The standard is simple, yet, how much liquor and the size of the pointer will influence the outcomes. That is the reason this strategy is a high level pouring method you want somewhat more practice.

CHAPTER SIX

SUPPLIES FOR FRACTAL DENDRITES POUR

• Isopropyl liquor

• Pointer (they accompany dirt apparatuses some of the time) - you can pick various sizes.

• Better use acrylic paint ink rather than standard paint or fluid paint.

• On the off chance that you're making exceptionally huge dendrites, you might require a pipette.

• Silicone.

THE MOST EFFECTIVE METHOD TO POUR FRACTAL DENDRITES

1. Premix with pouring medium and spread the foundation tone (negative tone) over the material.

2. Pour a full pipette of acrylic ink variety you like.

3. In the focal point of the acrylic ink circle, put 1 drop of silicone oil.

4. Next, add 1 drop of Isopropyl liquor.

5. Wait, be patient and watch the cycle start! On the off chance that the interaction appears to be excessively delayed for you, add more drops of liquor.

Supplies:

• 1 Teaspoons Titanium White paint I utilize fundamental Amsterdam Titanium White acrylic paint

• Liquitex Stream Help Medium

• 4 drops Liquitex Acrylic Ink (assuming you have it)

• 1/2 Teaspoon Elmers Paste All

• Do-It-Yourself Cell and binding activator

• Do-It-Yourself pouring medium:

• Half Behr Shiny Inside Profound base (or another profound base) + 25% Minwax Polycrylic + 25% Jo Sonja Stain, OR

• Only 3 sections Behr Inside Shiny Polish - Profound Base to 1 section Polycrylic

• 1 piece of Minwax Polycrylic with 1 piece of pouring medium

• Pipettes

• Acrylic paint colors you might want to utilize

• Gloves

• Light

For the main layer (pad or cushion)

1. The first layer is purported "pad" or "cushion", we for the most part use Titanium white blended in with Elmers Paste in proportion 1:1.

2. You may have to add a smidgen of water, yet don't over dilute the combination it ought to be still thick.

How much paint do you really want for the pad layer? For a 15×15 cm material, you'll require 100-120 ml of "pad".

For pouring medium (3 choices)

1. The most straightforward recipe: Blend 1 piece of Minwax Polycrylic in with 1 piece of pouring medium. Or then again

2. 50% Behr Reflexive Inside Profound base (or another profound base) + 25% Minwax Polycrylic + 25% Jo Sonja Stain OR

3. Just 3 sections Behr inside Reflexive Veneer - Profound Base to 1 section Polycrylic

For acrylic pour paint

1. Mix acrylic paint with Pouring medium in proportion 1 section to 3 sections in individual cups. It ought to be smooth and stream, yet ought to be essentially as liquid as standard pouring paint.

For Lacings and cells

1. Mix Liquitex Stream Help Medium with Titanium white until the paint begin dribbling gradually, as yet being very thick.

STEP BY STEP INSTRUCTIONS TO DO SHELEE CRAFTSMANSHIP SPROUT DUTCH POUR BINDING

1. Apply the pad layer and allow it to sit on the material, thick, don't spread it over material. It ought to sit in one spot.

2. Working quick, drop some of first tone, then, at that point, second tone, etc, until, the last tone. You want to contemplate how varieties will team up, yet sit back and relax it can come after some time with experience.

3. Ass binding blend, only 1-2 drops.

4. Start blowing utilizing only your mouth or a straw. Try not to catastrophe for hard and don't blow the pad layer, just the variety layers!

5. If you need more cells, use in the middle between "blowing" meeting.

6. Once you done blowing and making cells, begin shifting the material.

23 - Inflatable Crush Acrylic Pouring Strategy

The Ballon Crush acrylic pouring strategy is in a real sense what it seems like: you make an example with a swelled inflatable! This pouring strategy makes generally blossoms the same plans or dynamic pours and effectively can be joined with Filthy pour.

Additional provisions: inflatable's!

CHAPTER SEVEN

THE MOST EFFECTIVE METHOD TO DO INFLATABLE CRUSH POUR

1. Premix tones with pouring medium.

2. Apply foundation (negative) variety and spread it over the material.

3. Pour varieties on the material utilizing your 1 strategy: Puddle pour or Grimy Cup.

4. Inflate an inflatable! Not to an extreme, very much like a little ball (the size of the ball will direct the size of your example, so you can undoubtedly control it or expand a few unique inflatables).

5. Press the ballon against each poured puddle tenderly or with pressure attempt it first to see which results you like more. The harder you press the bigger plan will be and the more impacts you'll have.

On the other hand

1. Premix tones with pouring medium.

2. Pour the foundation tone.

3. Then take a plate and make puddles there. Not on the material!

4. Inflate the ballon.

5. Dip the inflatable in a puddle, then, at that point, move the example onto the material and continue to go that way! For

this reason this method is additionally called "swell plunge pour".

You can continuously go further and utilize silicone to make cells or straw to make blows.

24 - Plunging pour

Another plunging acrylic pouring method is a Plunge or Plunging pour. It is in fact the situation when we dunk the material in the paint, so it is a seriously confounded and progressed pour procedure, I trust you'll like.

Additional provisions:

• A plastic sheet or a shallow plate (somewhat bigger than the material you need to paint onto)

INSTRUCTIONS TO DO PLUNGING POUR

1. Premix all tones in individual cups.

2. Apply the tones onto the sheet or plate utilizing any fundamental strategy you need. Not on the material!

3. Now the plunging part: flip around you material and profound it in the plate.

4. Let is splash the paint for 3-10 sec and lift it up delicately.

5. You can rehash the stage 3 however many times as you wish!

25 - Colander Pour - Kaleidoscope liquid canvas method

Colander pour is utilized to make kaleidoscope impacts, and as you might figure we will involve a basic colander for it!

This is certainly not an extremely challenging acrylic pouring strategy, yet it does a WOW-impact without a doubt!

Additional provisions: mysterious colander!

INSTRUCTIONS TO DO COLANDER POUR

1. Premix your varieties with pouring medium and get them in a single cup, as for Messy pour.

2. Place the colander (perfect and dry!) in the focal point of the material.

3. Pour the paint in the colander with roundabout movements continue to pour until all paint will emerge.

4. Now paint will arrive at the openings and begin pouring onto the material, heads up!

5. Start lifting the colander gradually straight up and hold it up until all tones emerge. Try not to lift up excessively high it will be not so much as 1 inch up.

6. Set the colander to the side. We don't require it any longer.

7. In the focal point of your material you ought to now see the popular kaleidoscope impact!

8. Now beginning shifting your material delicately to spread the paint across.

26 - Pipe pour

The pipe pour stays in the kitchen devices segment, similar to a colander pour.

With Pipe pour we going to utilize a channel to get astounding cells and dazzling impacts, I guarantee!

Additional provisions: a basic channel.

For any acrylic pouring procedure I would propose utilizing a different channel, colander, or whatever other device that may possibly contact our food. Acrylics are not food protected and regardless of whether we clean all devices completely, I would in any case keep leisure activity and food discrete.

INSTRUCTIONS TO DO PIPE POUR

1. Premix all varieties you might want to use in individual cups, in addition to a negative tone (dark, white) in another cup.

2. Pour and spread the foundation tone.

3. Place the pipe over the material.

4. Start pouring paints individually, not all the cup, simply layering it pleasantly. Better pour all tones from one side of the channel.

5. Once you done, somewhat lift the channel up and begin hauling it around the material. The paint will stream on the canvas surface similar to the pipe has a tail. You can shape lines or circles, it depends on you!

6. Once the pipe is unfilled, you can include more paint the edges of the example.

7. Tilt. Furthermore, goodness, it is so lovely!

8. You can blow edges with a straw, light cells and even swipe on the off chance that you might want to try!

27 - Wave pour

One of the most famous acrylic pouring methods is the Wave pour so gorgeous and helps us to remember the sea, how it feels, how it sounds and the warm water contacts us. Wave pour causes disturbances, however it doesn't mean it generally ought to be sea blue, you can utilize any variety blends you need. The Wave acrylic pouring procedure might appear as though a variety of the Swipe pour as well, as we will require something to drag the paint to shape a wave.

Additional provisions: something to swipe (enormous range blade, paper towel, cardboard, plastic sheet, and so forth)

CHAPTER EIGHT

STEP BY STEP INSTRUCTIONS TO DO WAVE POUR

1. Premix all tones with pouring medium in individual cups.

2. Pour and spread the foundation tone, in the event that you're doing the exemplary wave it will be white.

3. Before you do the wave, sketch it to you, place it: where it ought to be? It is critical to be aware as you we begin pouring as indicated by it.

4. Start pouring more obscure tones where the lower part of the wave will be there the water is hazier. Most likely it will be the

lower part of the material too, simply pour one dim variety starting with one side then onto the next and same with different tones, you'd consider as dull and emulating profound water.

5. On one side, pour light tone (it very well may be dark, white with metallic), its where the wave begins to have some froth. Ordinarily, it will be one side of the material some place in this side.

6. So far it seems as though a wave, don't go nuts!

7. Now it is the main second, we are beginning hauling a cardboard or a wet towel from the lower part of the wave to the top, mimicking wave shape. You can utilize a range blade too.

8. Repeat stage 7 until you're content with how your wave seems to be. After each swipe stand by somewhat, so the paint will show the impact better, and afterward continue.

28 - Infusion pour (otherwise known as Mixture pour) with a needle

I've never known about this acrylic pour procedure previously, so I began my exploration. Infusion pour (likewise called implantation pour) utilizes a needle to sort of infuse the material with liquid paint.

However, not all recordings you will find under the Infusion pour label will have a needle, some of them will seem as though a puddle pour or some likeness thereof, so

INSTRUCTIONS TO DO INFUSION POUR/IMPLANTATION POUR

1. Premix your tones with pouring medium.

2. Flood your material with a foundation tone, let it sit in the center, don't spread.

3. Close the tip of the needle with your finger and layer the paint colors in the needle.

4. Take off the finger and set the needle in the focal point of the foundation tone. Gradually press and let the paint emerge from the needle, it will come out basically

under your experience tone and you will see the way the varieties fire springing up.

5. Once the needle is vacant, you are allowed to shift the material at this point!

On the other hand, the infusion should be possible just with liquid paint bottles: you put the principal variety first, and afterward you simply infuse it with bottle covers with various tones.

29 - Internet pour

Internet pour procedure makes entrancing internetbing impacts on the artistic creation surface. You will utilize a crush jug to make a trap of various varieties on a superficial level.

A few specialists say that this strategy is equivalent to Infusion pour (or Mixture pour), however I consider Infusion pour like one with a needle, so I will just momentarily survey the Internet pour as well.

Others see Internet pour as a variety of the Fractal Dendrites pouring strategy. I don't have the foggiest idea who is correct, for me a internet it's a cobinternet and I'll go with it.

The principal trouble with Internet pour is that we don't actually control the outcomes and it might become testing to get the ideal internet you need.

30 - Multi-Material Pour

Indeed, presently we go next level and we will pour at the few materials simultaneously.

The multi-material pour is great for making matching pour artistic creations and has no extra paint!

The fundamental guideline of a multi-material pour is that we stack a few materials like a pyramid, one on top of another, then we pour paint over the top material and let it stream down and flood materials under.

Supplies:

• A few materials (enormous - more modest - littlest)

• You'll need to premix more paint, as we will cover a few surfaces.

• Lift stands or additional cups for raising materials.

THE MOST EFFECTIVE METHOD TO DO MULTI-MATERIAL POUR

1. Premix the varieties as though you will do a Filthy cup pour

2. Stack the materials:

• The biggest at the base,

• The following one - more modest and raised (utilize extraordinary stands or simply plastic cups flipped around)

• The best one - the littlest material.

• It is ideal to stack them like a pine tree, not straight one under another however the two different ways are fine.

THE MOST EFFECTIVE METHOD TO STACK MATERIALS FOR MULTI-MATERIAL POUR

3. Start pouring premixed paint over the top material. Allow all paint to go down till the base material.

4. Once you done pouring, take off materials from this pyramid, slant every single one of them and allowed them to dry.

Or on the other hand course, you can paint various materials simultaneously without making a heap, you can continuously layer them one close to another and work logically on all painting surfaces.

31 - Two cup pour (Twofold cup pouring method)

The two-cup pour method is straightforward: to make a pouring work of art we will require two cups and these cups will be one inside another blast!

You ought to pick one more modest cup and one greater one and for this strategy, the estimating cups with a handle are better. This strategy is additionally called twofold cup pouring.

Supplies

• Two cups with handle (it is not difficult to get a bunch of 3 cups they are continuously coordinating and have greater and more modest sizes).

INSTRUCTIONS TO DO TWO CUP POUR

1. Premix your paint with pouring medium.

2. Fill around 50% of the large cup with layered paint (or less, depending on how

profound the more modest cup can fit it in the greater one).

3. Fill the little cup with layerd paint.

4. Put the little cup inside the huge cup their top edge ought to be on a similar level (that is the reason is smarter to get a set, as they are coordinating).

5. Now the troublesome aspect, pouring the paint. There are multiple ways of getting it done:

• Put the material on top of the cups (one inside another) and turn it over.

• Flip the two cups like for Flip cup pouring strategy (very troublesome).

• Simply pour moving the cups in small circles like for Tree Rings pour.

6. Carefully eliminate the cups.

7. Tilt, add more paint, light for additional cells, do as you wish in all actuality do obtain ideal outcome.

32 - Sledge pour

Hammer pour is certainly not an exceptionally famous new acrylic pouring method. Hammer pour is the point at which we pour and sprinkle paint on a hard composition surface (material will be excessively delicate).

We can utilize a gesso board or a wooden board and a sledge or hammer.

Supplies:

• Hard canvas surface (wooden board). Assuming that you pick wood, ensure you will prime it first, any other way, paint won't stick as expected.

• An elastic hammer is an optimal decision.

INSTRUCTIONS TO DO SLEDGE POUR

1. Cover your functioning region with plastic and wear a cover (this method is chaotic)

2. Premix your acrylic paint with pouring medium.

3. Spread the foundation variety over the work of art surface.

4. Using Puddle pours or customary pours pour the paint over (go ahead and try different things with some other fundamental acrylic pouring method as a base for Sledge pour).

5. Take a mallet and make sprinkles! Continue onward, adding paint and sprinkling until you like the outcomes. The harder you hit the more sprinkles you get.

POUR PAINTING PROCEDURES FAQ

What are the various kinds of acrylic pouring strategies?

I vary acrylic pouring procedures by level: for novices and progressed. Novices' pouring strategies don't include unique information or any additional provisions (extra costs), they are basic and speedy. High level acrylic pouring procedures require more practice, persistence, and here and there extra pouring devices or even an exceptional recipe.

The fundamental acrylic pouring methods for fledglings are Puddle pour, Flip cup, Dutch pour.

High level acrylic pouring procedures are String Pour, Marble Pour, Blossom pour, Swipe pour, Shelee Workmanship Dutch pour, Fractal Dendrites pour, and some more.

Peruse too: 25 Acrylic Painting Strategies For Novices to Paint like a Genius

What is the best acrylic pour method?

For my purposes, the most dynamite, the best, acrylic pour procedure is essential Dutch pour perfect impacts just with paint and a hairdryer! I additionally like lovely cells with the Swipe procedure and the straightforwardness of the Flip cup pour strategy simply blend the paint and go!

The best procedure for pouring for me is a blend! You can continuously add air, cells, make designs with a channel. Simply have some good times!

How would you get great cells in acrylic pouring?

The fundamental fixing to get great cells in acrylic pouring is great silicone oil.

100 percent silicone oil is the most ideal decision: Impresa Pouring oil for huge cells or Impresa Silicone oil for numerous more modest cells.

What is the equation for acrylic pouring?

Acrylic pouring depends on a decent recipe on the grounds that the paint stream is required for good outcomes. The best recipe for acrylic pouring is to blend 1 piece of Floetrol in with 2 pieces of the acrylic paint. Add then 2 to 4 drops of silicone oil to make decent cells.

One more famous recipe for acrylic pouring is to blend half Floetrol, 30% paint, and 20% water, and afterward add silicone oil.

How would you manage extra acrylic pour paint?

You can utilize it to paint with! The consistency will be exceptionally high stream yet the paint will appear straightforward. You can likewise utilize extra paint to pour on a few little items, for example, rocks, shells bits of wood, or other little articles. Premixed acrylic pours paint can remain great for a couple of days on the off chance that you will appropriately close the top.

ACRYLIC PAINT POURING INVESTIGATING

What do I do on the off chance that the paint sitting on material and not exactly moving? Have a go at adding really spilling medium to disperse paint more.

Imagine a scenario in which my paint pouring is running off the material excessively fast. Add less pouring medium and more paint to thicken the blend.

Consider the possibility that I pour my paint on the material and the paint doesn't over the material all of way. Take a stab at stirring up a greater amount of the paint combination and pour in the region where the paint hasn't covered. A delightful aspect concerning paint pouring sister how each painting is unique. Consider the possibility that I could do without my poured painting. You have several choices! Assuming that your paint pouring is as yet wet, you can scratch the paint off and attempt once more. In the event that it's dry or too dry to even consider eliminating, basically stir up a new clump of pouring medium/paint combination and does a new paint pour over a similar material, it will cover it up. For what reason does my paint pouring has a ton of air pockets? Rises in paint pouring can have been on the grounds that it was over blended, or stirred up prior to utilizing.

While your cost is as yet wet, you can attempt delicately tapping on the underside of your work of art while keeping it level to bring any air pockets up to the surface. In the event that you feel like the air pockets are all up, you can cautiously utilize a toothpick to pop the air pockets too. In the event that your paint poured piece is now dry, prior to applying the unmistakable coat, you can have a go at taking a flimsy brush with a matching tone and paint over the air pocket.

THE END

www.ingramcontent.com/pod-product-compliance
Lightning Source LLC
Chambersburg PA
CBHW062347290526
45794CB00005B/2124